Bridges of Dreams

A Journey of Hope and Triumph in New Lands

Jaime Guevara

Dedication

For my dear readers, who breathe life into these pages and give my words the chance and power to change the world.

To my wife, children, grandchildren, and through all generations of time, thank you for letting this book inspire you to overcome challenges and succeed in life.

Acknowledgment

First and foremost, praise and thanks to my Heavenly Father, the Almighty, for his showers of blessings throughout the development of my book until its completion. I want to infinitely thank my Heavenly Father, who inspired and guided me through the Holy Ghost to write this book and share it with all the people in the world. For years, I wanted to be the author of my own book and share my successes, challenges, and constant overcoming of the difficulties in life to achieve something better for my personal and family well-being.

Through sharing this book, I want to inspire, motivate, and encourage people so that we can be a happy and self-sufficient family and be able to change the world with actions of peace, harmony, love, and mutual respect.

I want to thank the love of my life, Fortu Guevara, my wife, who has been one of my biggest inspirations to do this book and has been so emotionally and economically supportive over all the years since she came to the USA.

I always knew that you believed in me and let me spend more time doing my book while you were cleaning the house, preparing my food, washing my clothes, shopping for food, and doing other things in the house while I was working on my book with ideas, details, rough drafts, and recordings.

I want to thank my children, Lila and Nefi Guevara, for being part of this book. They shared their educational experiences and graduation photos from college with me and obeyed the advice from their parents based on our example. Also, I want my children to know they are my greatest accomplishment. I admire and adore them both.

I want to thank my father, Máximo Guevara, who planted the seed of knowledge in my mind and nurtured it by providing his extraordinary example of studying, working, and achieving a university degree that opened the doors to great economic and social opportunities for the well-being of us, his children, and the entire family.

I want to thank my mother, Gumercinda Bocanegra de Guevara, for being an extraordinary and masterful example with high moral and spiritual values. My Mom deserves a lot of credit for always encouraging and motivating me to do the best in my life. Her drive and determination to make the world a better place are contagious. I love you very much

About the Author

Jaime Guevara's life story is a tale of resilience, family legacy, and the transformative power of education. Born in 1968 in Lima, Peru, Guevara's path was marked early on by academic excellence, with him graduating as the valedictorian of his high school class.

Driven by a deep-rooted passion for health and biological sciences that ran through his family's lineage, Guevara made the courageous decision to immigrate to the United States, steadfastly pursuing a better life for his loved ones. Despite the challenges of separation and bureaucratic hurdles, Guevara's unwavering determination ultimately reunited him with his wife and children, setting the stage for an inspiring chapter of familial collaboration and academic achievement.

Undeterred by adversity, Guevara embarked on a touching journey, earning his biological sciences degree alongside his daughter—a profoundly meaningful experience that strengthened their bond and ignited their shared dream of graduating from dental school.

Though fate dealt a setback when Guevara's wife could no longer work due to injury, Guevara's resolute spirit and his family's unwavering support propelled him forward, prioritizing his daughter's dental education and his son's higher education before ultimately realizing his own aspirations.

Guevara's legacy extends beyond his personal triumphs, as both of his children have followed in his footsteps, with his eldest daughter graduating from dentistry school and his son earning a degree in biomedical sciences. This intergenerational pursuit of excellence is a testament to the power of leading by example and the transformative potential of education.

Through his captivating memoir, Guevara invites readers to embark on an unforgettable odyssey that celebrates the indomitable human spirit, the enduring strength of family bonds, and the life-changing impact of a relentless commitment to learning and growth. His story inspires all those who dare to dream of a better future, reminding us that with unwavering determination and faith, the most formidable obstacles can be overcome.

Contents

Introduction: Seeds of Aspiration

We are all born with a dream, a willingness to pursue what we aim for. Some of us settle for more, others for less. Nonetheless, we are born into the world with a divine purpose.

Students worldwide study and aim to become engineers, lawyers, businessmen, and doctors. Every dream comes with its own set of sacrifices and troubles, and no path is easy to take—the key to achieving what you want lies in working hard.

I want to share my story with you because many like me have traveled the paths and lost their way in the middle. One tends to give up in the face of adversity, but I want my truth to be an example that propels you and your family in your journey toward your dreams.

I believe this story will resonate with every person who has gone through hurdles in life. My and my family's journey has been marked by sacrifices that have shaped us into who we are today.

You can overcome whatever life throws at you with power, love, and belief in your strength and passion.

In the depths of our family's history lies a story of sacrifice and unbreakable bonds that have held us together over time.

This is a memoir, a testament to the struggles that have shaped us, and a reminder that our stories are forever intertwined with our dreams.

Dear reader, the seeds of aspirations are already planted within you. However, it takes years of determination, resilience, and patience to receive the outcome and harvest the fruit.

I hope you know there is no limit to what you wish to aim for. *There is no barrier impossible to cross.*

Chapter 1: Early Education and Challenges In Peru

"Corruption in education leads to some people getting highly educated, and then these people support the uneducated to rule over the illiterate masses."

-Amit Abraham.

A new chapter of my life unfolded when I graduated from high school and delved into the complexities of the fiercely competitive world of academics.

College admissions were about to begin, and I was preparing for the challenges of passing admission tests. It took me a year to study diligently, and I was adamant about reaching new heights in my career. My determination was fueled by the desire to excel in my academic pursuits, but I wasn't aware of the hurdles I had to face.

In the heart of Peru, the tradition brought students together nationwide. Lima, the capital, became the center of attention, attracting hopeful individuals from all directions who came to seek opportunities for higher education. The stakes to be enrolled in the best universities were high, and the competition was tough.

With distinction and the honor of being one of the top graduates, I passed high school with flying colors. The road to my success was supposed to be clear-cut, but that wasn't the case. Typically, the top two graduated students in high school were exempt from the rigorous admission tests. My happiness knew no bounds because this opportunity would allow me to get into medical college, saving me from the strict admission test thousands of candidates had to compete for.

Suddenly, corruption came in the way of my path, detouring me away from the traditional merit-based route. I was denied the privilege of direct admission and had no choice but to join the competition against other students and secure my seat. The admission board, which carried out admission tests, received money from parents to admit less-qualified students into medical colleges, and the merit system was nowhere to be found. It was all due to the unjustified impact of commercial transactions; parents could secure a slot for their children by paying a higher fee, regardless of their child's academic performance.

The Universidad Nacional Federico Villarreal in Lima, Perú

Despite the roadblocks, I was determined to pursue my goals. I continued my journey and applied to medical college at the Universidad Nacional Federico Villarreal in Lima, Peru. Around 3,000 to 4,000 hopeful students gathered at the doorstep to take the test, but there weren't enough seats for the honor roll students. Eventually, many high-achievers like myself were relocated to other majors offered by the university. Our seats were given to the students who could pay well.

Those who studied hard for the medical test felt betrayed by the unfair justice system backed up by the corrupted admission board. My dream of enrolling in a medical college seemed miles away from coming true.

The revelation of this systemic injustice dealt a devastating blow to my aspirations, challenging the very foundations of academic integrity. Despite my steadfast commitment to earning success through merit, I was entangled in a web of deceit.

My parents instilled the value of earning success through academic excellence. Still, the harsh reality revealed a disheartening truth—financial support played a decisive role, particularly in securing seats in medical colleges. It surprised me and left me with no choice but to look for an alternate route.

With a heavy heart, I decided to pursue psychology as my major. Luckily, the college I applied to recognized my potential as an honor roll student. They enrolled me immediately, and I spent over two years studying psychology.

Nonetheless, my passion for medical school remained, resembling a fire that could never be put out. Inside my heart, I still wanted to pursue my dreams— I was still looking for opportunities to get into medical school.

Undeterred by adversity, the opportunity for an "Internal Transfer" appeared when I was almost 20 years old. The chance of transferring my psychology major to medical school was a glimmer of newfound hope.

But even that was not a guaranteed ticket to medical school either. Many students, like myself, were competing for a seat in medical college while majoring in something different, including psychology. The struggle continued, and once again, it seemed like those whose parents paid the higher price had the upper hand.

In that contest for admission, the unfair pattern repeated. The students with financial support secured spots, while others, like me and my parents, stood firm on earning opportunities through our hard work.

Even though I was one of the brightest and most promising candidates hoping to enter medical school, I held onto my parent's beliefs. It became a challenge to navigate through a system where merit seemed to be overshadowed by financial influence.

After witnessing the injustice I faced, my mother was fueled by her determination. She managed to secure an appointment with the president of the medical school, a feat that was neither common nor easy for parents at the time. Her perseverance and perhaps a bit of good fortune made the meeting with the president possible.

During the meeting, she elaborated on my achievements in high school and presented my academic records before him to demonstrate my potential as a deserving candidate for medical school. The president recognized my abilities and extended a lifeline toward my dreams. He expressed sympathy and acknowledged the injustice of the situation, which gave me the validation I needed.

This encounter marked a turning point for me, as it seemed that someone in authority finally understood the challenges I faced that had hindered my path to medical school. Ultimately, he facilitated my acceptance into the medical college, and I was determined to overcome the obstacles that were to come.

I began my journey into medical school and studied diligently. I read through textbooks and attended classes regularly, ensuring nothing could stop me from becoming a doctor. However, throughout the year, external factors plagued my academic pursuits.

I only studied for one year in medical school, as each semester took nearly a year to complete due to frequent strikes. These strikes were initiated by more advanced students and often involved professors protesting for better pay.

The medical college was plagued by internal power struggles, with different factions competing for authority, much like the Democrats and Republicans in the United States. These conflicts led to frequent strikes, sometimes lasting three to four months, during which the college was temporarily closed. After each strike, the college would reopen briefly, allowing us to resume our studies for a few weeks before another strike would occur. This cycle extended one semester of studies into a year, prolonging what should have been a standard academic year into a drawn-out ordeal.

As I approached the end of my first year, I realized how difficult it would be to finish my medical education under these conditions. Unlike private institutions, the national university was subject to constant disruptions, making it nearly impossible to complete my studies on time.

Simultaneously, my personal life was evolving. I met my wife during my first year in medical school, and we had our first child in the same year. I embraced parenthood with open arms, and within a few months, we welcomed our beautiful daughter into the world.

Amid the chaos of prolonged education, fatherhood added a new sense of responsibility to my shoulders. I knew I needed to provide for my family one way or another. But, in Peru, jobs for younger individuals offered minimum wages, which meant raising a family was difficult, even if both partners worked.

The harsh truth dawned upon me that raising a family and pursuing medicine would be difficult for me, given the circumstances that we were facing in Peru.

I contemplated moving abroad because my sister, a pioneer and an inspiration to our family, had already been in the United States since 1978. She applied for my mother to become a resident, and later, my mother extended the opportunity for permanent residence to my brothers and me. In Peru, my future was uncertain, and I needed to consider an alternative route where I could begin again with my family.

The decision to move to the United States in 1993 was daunting and terrifying initially, but with resilience and positivity, I was ready to move ahead. This path provided relief from the challenging circumstances in Peru.

Chapter 2: Journey Across Borders

"The only limit to our realization of tomorrow will be our doubts of today."

-Franklin D. Roosevelt.

In 1993, with a permanent resident visa in hand, I began a journey that would forever change the trajectory of my life. Despite the struggles and adversities of moving to the United States, I still remember the first day my flight landed on American soil. It was 3 November, and I had packed my bags, ready to leave my old life behind.

Regardless of what others say, moving to another country is always a deeply personal experience; one is never prepared for what is to come. Not only was I starting a new chapter in the United States, but I was also moving across the lands into different cultures and languages.

I was leaving behind the life I knew, traveling away from my homeland, hoping for a brighter future.

With the circumstances that made me leave Peru, it was inevitable—I would have to spend many years away from my family.

Moving abroad to the United States represented a land of endless possibilities, where dreams could be transformed into reality through hard work and determination. However, nothing could prepare me for the road that lay ahead. I had to stay apart from my family for seven long years before reuniting with them. Deciding to live apart for such an extended period was one of the most challenging decisions my wife and I ever made.

The pain and heartbreak of being in a long distance with my wife and my child was excruciating. Living apart came with its own set of frustrations. There were several days and nights that my wife and I spent crying, trying our best to stay connected and make the most of our lives.

The driving force propelling me forward was the hope that my family could live under one roof again, but time would take its course.

My wife's constant support became the backbone that strengthened me through the seven long years of wait. Reaching the mountain top required initial steps, and we still had a long way to go before my family would enter the United States as immigrants. Together, we were determined to soar through the difficulties.

El Charro Restaurant, where I worked taking orders.

During this time, I had to remain patient and work diligently to ensure financial stability and make ends meet. Eventually, the loneliness of living alone crept in, and my heart yearned to reunite with my family. I decided to fill the years leading up to our reunion with relentless hard work.

Apart from my long-term aspirations for my family, my mind was occupied with one goal: I wanted my wife and daughter with me as soon as possible. Every single process for their immigration required me to earn well; saving money was essential to welcoming my family with open arms.

I was willing to do everything possible to bring my family to the United States of America. Trips, immigration applications, and housing required a stable income, but I had to start small like every immigrant. Instead of fixating on a permanent job, I decided to work at various places and save up for my plans.

Nothing could be achieved without resilience, and hard work was the only way out, so I began my first job as a busboy, then took orders in a Mexican restaurant.

While taking orders, I realized the vast cultural differences and language barriers. This job not only paid well but also served as an opportunity to polish my English skills by talking to various customers. With a newfound desire for personal and professional development, my mindset brimmed with positivity. Working in a new place and adjusting to another country's way of living was tough, but I knew anything was possible— I just had to go at it with full force.

Eventually, I was eager to build my English language skills. So, I enrolled at Georgia State University, Atlanta, for two years. Regular classes and experienced professors helped me immerse myself in grammar, syntax, and vocabulary.

As time passed, learning English as a second language became the reason I gained the confidence to speak, write, and read in the States. With a newfound motivation, my days were spent finding better opportunities to propel me toward my goals. There was still plenty of time before my family migrated, and I was eager to find the means to provide for them.

After finishing my English classes at Georgia State University, I stumbled upon an opportunity to work as a lead man for several warehouse and manufacturing companies. This job helped me use my advanced skills in communication, paving the way for me to assist the supervisors in their tasks.

With relentless enthusiasm, I embraced every opportunity to learn and grow. I was eager to develop new skills and take on various jobs to reach my goals and dreams. Gradually, I worked tirelessly and started saving money to move toward my aspirations. Each small accomplishment fueled my determination to work even harder. As my savings grew, so did my self-confidence, bringing me one step closer to achieving my dreams. With every passing day, I felt a sense of pride and fulfillment, knowing that my hard work and perseverance were paving the way to a brighter future.

A few months later, I started working as a punch-out maker for a residential home builder. My job consisted of utilizing my handyman skills to ensure that newly constructed homes were perfectly finished. This included caulking, touch-up painting, and repairing cabinets and vanity doors. A lot of my time was spent completing drywall repairs, installing doors and knobs, and hanging pictures, mirrors, and shelves. From adjusting electrical cover plates, outlets, and light fixtures, I was able to tackle a variety of tasks.

This hands-on experience equipped me with the knowledge and skills to handle many home improvement tasks efficiently and effectively.

Elks Aidmore in Conyers, GA, where I worked as a residential maintenance technician.

Gaining experience as a punch-out worker landed me a job on a government-funded construction project, which proved very valuable. I began to work for the Conyers Housing Authority as a maintenance technician.

One of the houses of Conyers Housing Authority, where I worked as a residential maintenance technician.

The government agency allowed me to enroll in residential, electrical, and plumbing classes. In this role, I performed routine maintenance and repairs on various properties, including plumbing, electrical, and HVAC systems. I also conducted inspections to identify potential issues and implemented preventive measures to ensure the safety and functionality of the properties.

Photo of my wife and two children living in Peru while I lived alone in the USA.

During these seven years, many days were filled with trials and tribulations. However, my goal to reunite with my family kept me going. Every day, the hope to bridge the gap between my wife and children kept me afloat. Meanwhile, my wife stayed busy in Peru, taking care of our daughter and actively participating in church activities, which provided her with a strong support network. Despite the distance and the lack of modern communication tools, we stayed connected through weekly phone calls and letters. Our shared faith in God and commitment to the Gospel helped us endure the long years of separation.

My wife and I remained steadfastly loyal to each other throughout, despite the temptations that naturally arose from prolonged separation.

We knew our sacrifices were for a greater purpose—to provide our children with better opportunities and a brighter future. Our love and commitment to each other were unwavering, and we supported each other through the challenges of our long-distance relationship.

During these years, I visited my family in Peru once a year. Traveling back home brought immense joy and sorrow in equal measure. The brief moments we spent together were filled with happiness, but leaving them behind each time was heart-wrenching. Each visit, however, reaffirmed our decision and strengthened our resolve to achieve our goal of a better life in the United States. The memories of those visits sustained me, providing the emotional strength to face each day alone in a foreign land.

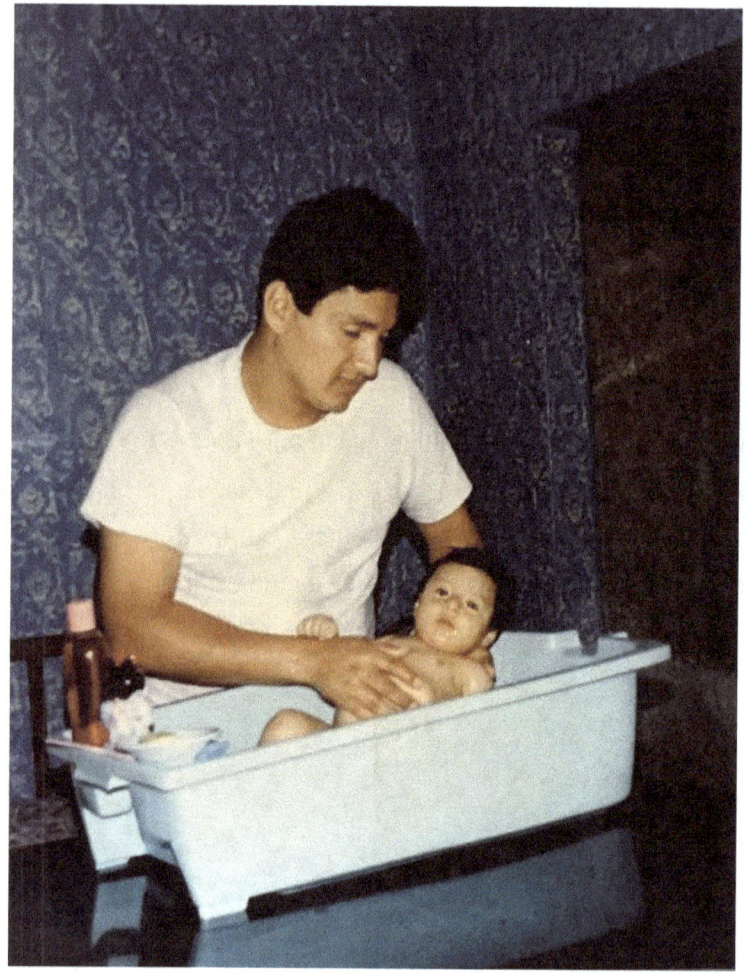

In 1996, my son was born, but unfortunately, I could not be there for his birth. I was ecstatic to meet my baby boy, and the agony of being away from him tugged at my heart. Eventually, I planned to fly to Peru a week later to visit him.

The happiness of holding my newborn son was a feeling that couldn't be described in words. Every sacrifice began to seem worthwhile.

Despite the joy, the goodbyes were immensely heartbreaking. But I was determined to pursue the goals and dreams I had envisioned for my family.

The pain of separation renewed my motivation to work toward the goals and dreams I had envisioned for myself and my family.

I missed the comfort of being home and yearned to reunite with my family. My wife managed everything in Peru, and my kids grew up without me. For this reason, I worked and studied hard every day from Monday to Sunday one week and Monday to Saturday the next.

Visiting my family in Peru. Photo of my two children with me.

My focus was on acquiring diverse skills and expanding my knowledge and wisdom to ensure my family's financial stability upon arriving in the United

States of America. I was driven to provide my wife and children a better life in the States, even if it meant facing the struggles alone for seven long years.

The painful memories and the loneliness were worth it—*everything would fade away when I would hug my wife and hold my kids in my arms.*

Chapter 3: Family Reunion and Life in The U.S.

"The best way out is always through."

-Robert Frost.

After five years of adapting and working tirelessly, I proudly became a U.S. citizen in 1998. This accomplishment filled me with immense pride and a renewed sense of purpose, igniting a fresh hope for my family's future.

With my citizenship secured, I immediately set my sights on reuniting with my family. I meticulously filled out the necessary immigration applications to bring my wife and children to join me in the United States. The process was complex. Each day was marked by anticipation and the sincere hope that our family would soon be together again.

After seven years of waiting, the awaited day finally arrived— my wife received her permanent resident visa for the United States.

The anticipation was palpable; we counted down the days until we reunited.

My wife and our children at the airport in Lima, Peru. My wife was saying goodbye to our children cause she was coming to the USA for the first time. Our children stayed in Peru alone with my parents for one year before coming to the USA.

In 2001, my wife landed in the United States, and my happiness knew no bounds. The moment I was desperately yearning for the last seven years was now my reality. It felt like a dream come true.

It was a bittersweet moment to be reunited with my wife in the US after spending so much time apart. We kissed each other, and tears flowed.

When we saw each other, we ran toward one another. Her arms embraced me tightly. Sobs escaped our lips as tears streamed down our faces—the struggle of migrating to the States had been worth it.

However, we still had many roads to travel together. My wife had landed, but we still had to bring our kids to the United States.

The hectic bureaucratic procedures made it difficult for my family to migrate together. It meant we had to stay apart from our kids for at least one year.

My wife was the first to receive her permit, and she traveled alone to the United States with the plan that our children would follow shortly. However, complications arose at the American Embassy in Peru. Despite being assured by the immigration office in Atlanta that a single application for my wife would suffice for the entire family, the embassy insisted that separate applications were required for each child. This unexpected obstacle meant my children had to stay behind in Peru for another year, cared for by my parents until their paperwork was processed.

When my wife arrived, I showed her around, and we reminisced over the days we had spent without each other. Nothing could top the feeling that being with her brought forth. She found work in a pillow factory, and together, we worked tirelessly to build a stable life for our children. Each job and each hour of labor was a step closer to our dream of a united family and a better future.

Finally, in 2002, my children joined us in the United States, automatically gaining U.S. citizenship on my behalf. The joy of our reunion was indescribable, a culmination of years of sacrifice and unwavering hope. Seeing my whole family in our new home was a moment of profound happiness and relief.

Photo of our children, my wife, and I at the airport in Lima, Peru, ready to depart to the USA after waiting a year for the immigration approval to bring our children and finally to be together.

It was a difficult and emotionally taxing time for our family, but we remained resilient in our pursuit of bringing our loved ones together.

Eventually, our family reunited in the United States after a year of bureaucratic hurdles and waiting. The moment we were all together again was a joyous occasion filled with laughter, tears, and a deep sense of gratitude. We wasted no time adjusting to our new family dynamic, making small but meaningful changes to accommodate each other and strengthen our bond.

One of the challenges we faced was adjusting to living together as a family after years of separation. As someone who had lived alone for many years, I had developed certain habits and routines that needed to be modified now that my family was with me. Simple things like organizing belongings and household chores now became shared responsibilities, requiring patience and compromise.

Despite the initial adjustments, our family quickly found its rhythm, and we embraced our newfound togetherness with open arms. I took on the role of teaching English to my children, spending evenings and weekends to help them improve their language skills. It was a rewarding experience to see them progress and gain confident in their abilities with each passing day.

My son and I are in his elementary school in Conyers, GA, USA.

As my children settled into their new lives in the United States, they faced the challenge of adapting to a new school environment and making friends in a foreign land. My son, in particular, excelled in his studies and quickly became fluent in English, impressing his teachers and classmates alike. His adaptability and resilience were a source of pride for our family, and we celebrated each milestone he achieved.

Similarly, my daughter faced her own challenges but approached them with determination and grace. Despite being initially placed in an ESL (English as a Second Language) program, she wanted to join regular classes with native English speakers to accelerate her language learning. Her courage and initiative paid off, and she quickly became proficient in English, excelling academically and socially.

As parents, my wife and I provided unwavering support to our children, encouraging them to pursue their dreams and aspirations. We instilled in them the importance of education and hard work, setting an example by furthering our own education alongside them. Our commitment to academic excellence and personal growth laid the foundation for our children's success and future opportunities.

The journey to reunite our family in the United States was fraught with challenges and obstacles, but our unwavering determination and love for each other carried us through. By overcoming adversity together, we emerged stronger and more resilient as a family, ready to embrace the opportunities in our new home.

Our sacrifices were not in vain, as they paved the way for a better future— *a path we were determined to take.*

My daughter's graduation from High School in Conyers, GA, USA.

Chapter 4: Pursuing Higher Education

"Patience and perseverance have a magical effect before which difficulties disappear and obstacles vanish."

-John Quincy Adams

Before discussing my decision to major in Biology, I believe explaining my family's history in pursuing education is crucial.

In Peru, nearly 90% of my ancestors were deeply entrenched in scientific pursuits, with careers spanning various fields within science. From doctors to pharmacists, dentists to biologists, the lineage of scientific inquiry ran strong within my family.

This familial legacy laid the groundwork for my academic journey and my children's. Our collective interest in science, particularly within the medical and dental fields, steered us towards a shared goal of pursuing higher education as a family unit. Our aim was twofold: to further our knowledge and to establish a solid educational foundation for future generations in the United States.

The decision to major in Biology was strategic; my daughter and I were driven by our aspirations to apply to dental school. With unanimous agreement among family members, we dived headfirst into the academic pursuit with determination and dedication.

Georgia State University in downtown Atlanta, GA, from where I graduated in Biological Sciences.

My journey of academic excellence began at Georgia State University in Atlanta, where I took various foundational courses, from general studies to more specialized science subjects. Resuming my college education after a significant hiatus meant refreshing my memory of subjects I had previously studied in Peru. Adapting to the academic English vocabulary used in college courses presented another hurdle, but I knew that language was a skill I could learn through patience and perseverance.

Initially, it was difficult for me to adapt to the American education system. It was because the courses taught in the United States posed a greater difficulty than those taught in Peru.

However, with time and help from the University's exceptional teaching methods, I grasped the fundamental concepts of most subjects effortlessly, except U.S. history.

My entire life was spent in Peru, and I did not know enough about the history of the United States. With the lengthy curriculum to follow, I struggled to understand the details of the subject because it was entirely new to me.

My dedication to excel in U.S. history grew, so I indulged in studying for long hours. My entire focus was on mastering the subject matter. I read history books thoroughly to supplement my understanding of the material taught by the university professors.

My wife by her car, wearing the Golden State Food employee uniform, where she was an employee for several years. She helped me with the family income while I was studying in college.

Apart from other challenges, balancing the demands of academia with familial responsibilities was no easy feat. While my wife worked full-time, I juggled part-time employment with my rigorous school schedule, often rising before dawn to dedicate precious hours to study. Despite the fatigue that accompanied my limited sleep, I persevered, ensuring that education remained a top priority in my life.

Throughout the week, I could only get 8 hours of rest every Saturday. Our family gathered for church on Sundays, and weekdays were occupied with studies and intense working hours.

Eventually, I reached the point of exhaustion, but what kept me going was practicing discipline and following routines. Sacrifice was necessary to pursue my dreams and goals, and I was ready to face the challenges that life had in store for me. Quitting was not an option, so I gathered the bravery to push through.

Achieving a high grade point average required substantial effort, particularly in science courses requiring extensive memorization. Fortunately, my innate ability to memorize information quickly served me well, facilitating my academic success. I maintained exemplary grades, including numerous A's and A-pluses, which became the highlight of my academic journey.

My pursuit of a college education served as the cornerstone for future generations, laying the groundwork for our family's enduring legacy in the United States. Rooted in Peru yet aspiring to make America our new home, we recognized the importance of educational attainment in forging a brighter future. Our academic pursuits were not merely individual endeavors but collective efforts to secure a better life for ourselves and those who would follow in our footsteps.

This was just the beginning of success for the generations of Guevara's that were to come.

Chapter 5: From Biology to Dental Dreams

"Don't give up on your dreams, or your dreams will give up on you."

-John Wooden.

The passion to pursue my dreams was a constant driving force throughout my life because I firmly believed that gaining knowledge was a lifelong journey—one I was eager to continue with my beloved daughter.

Finally, my daughter and I graduated with a biology major on May 16, 2014. We achieved our goal of obtaining an undergraduate degree and were ready to expand upon our dreams. Both of us harbored the ambition to enroll in a prestigious dental school and make a meaningful impact in the world of dentistry.

My daughter and I were well aware that the field was highly competitive, and we knew that we had to be diligent in our studies, create meticulous schedules, and never miss a deadline. Our passions were intensified when we reflected upon our ultimate goal. We wanted to help others achieve optimal oral health and transform lives through the art of dental care. With unwavering dedication and unrelenting enthusiasm, we continued striving for excellence, ready to face the challenges of pursuing our dreams.

As we began applying to several dental schools throughout the states, my daughter took the DAT (Dental Admission Test), the standardized exam for admission to most dental schools in the United States. She passed the test on her first attempt and received a good score. When it was my turn to take the Dental Admission Test, our family was unexpectedly hit with hardship.

Just as I was about to implement my plans, my wife suffered severe shoulder pain due to a work-related injury in the past. The excruciating pain in her arm forced her to take a leave from work, suddenly thrusting the entire responsibility of our household onto my shoulders. As the sole breadwinner, I had to work tirelessly to support my family, taking on extra shifts and overtime to make ends meet. The financial burden was crushing, but I was committed to ensuring my family's well-being and security during this trying time.

I had to work diligently to provide my family with basic necessities such as food, clothing, medicine, education, and timely bill payments. Moreover, I supported my daughter's dental school applications, covering all the associated expenses. Despite the overwhelming challenges, my determination to keep our family afloat and create a brighter future for my loved ones kept me going.

With the weight of responsibilities on my mind, I postponed my dreams of pursuing dental education by canceling my applications to dental schools.

With a heavy heart, my focus was on prioritizing my family's needs over my own. However, I was determined not to let this setback define me. Once our financial burdens were alleviated, I would attempt the Dental Admission Test and pursue my dreams.

In a remarkable turn of events, my daughter received an interview invitation from the prestigious Dental College of Georgia and was subsequently accepted. This milestone reignited my passion for dental education, and I realized that our shared journey could catalyze something greater. My initial desire to pursue dental education alongside my daughter was rooted in the vision of establishing a family business in the science field, which would eventually grow into an economic empire, benefiting our family, extended family, and future generations.

As we continued this journey together, I knew our bond and shared purpose would strengthen. Moreover, our joint pursuit of dental education was driven by a deeper drive—to serve our community, particularly the underserved and marginalized. We aimed to provide essential dental services to low-income individuals, support the welfare of the needy, and positively impact the lives of the hungry, thirsty, poor, abandoned children, orphans, widows, disabled, and the sick. By doing so, we hoped to create a lasting legacy of compassion, empathy, and kindness.

My daughter and I were on our way to setting an example for generations to come.

Chapter 6: Overcoming Financial and Health Challenges

"It is during our darkest moments that we must focus to see the light."

-Aristotle.

As a family, we faced a particularly challenging period due to severe financial difficulties. The pain in my wife's shoulder, which had been persistent for an extended period, led to a series of medical appointments— agonizing and disabling her from continuing her activities of daily living.

The sharp, shooting pain in her affected shoulder was excruciating and intense. Soon enough, we decided to take her to the hospital again. Ultimately, the doctors requested an MRI scan, and we waited anxiously for her reports.

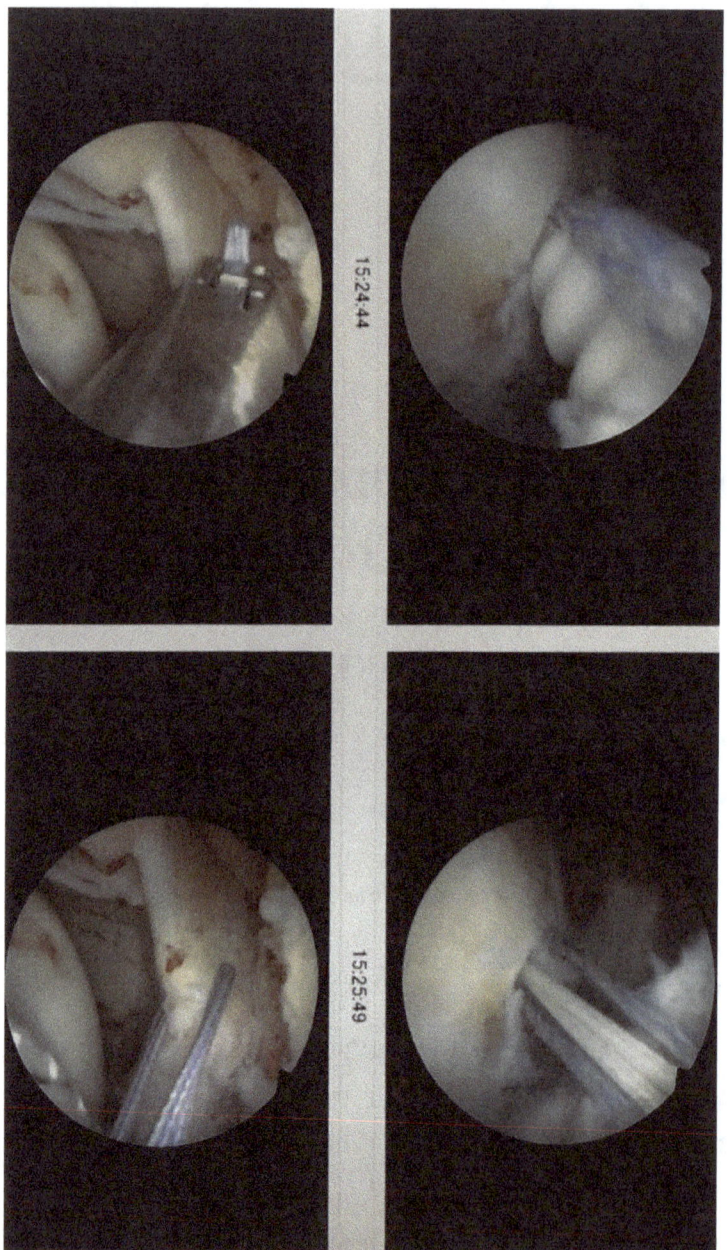

Photo of my wife's rotator cuff repair surgery due to an injury at work.

Once the reports arrived, we were shocked that the damage was much more severe than anticipated. The results revealed two completely ruptured tendons and one partially ruptured tendon, indicating immediate medical attention. The severity of the injury was such that conservative methods could no longer manage it, and therefore, the doctors suggested surgical repair of her right rotator cuff.

She underwent the procedure, and I was grateful for her surgery's success. However, my wife's post-operative recovery required a lengthy 12-month physical therapy program to ensure she could return to her daily life. During this time, the medical expenses of physiotherapy services were partially insured, and the medical bills skyrocketed. This, combined with our existing financial obligations, including mortgage payments, electricity, water, food, clothing, medicine, car insurance, gasoline, student loans, and other essential expenditures, significantly burdened our family's finances.

As time progressed, managing the finances alone was becoming increasingly difficult. My income was insufficient to cover these expenses, leading to a precarious financial situation. The pressure was mounting, and the weight of responsibility was falling on my shoulders.

To improve our financial stability, I set out to find other ways to earn an additional income. After thorough contemplation, my focus shifted to the technical skills I had gained as a handyman in America. Drawing on the experience acquired during my time in the real estate industry, specifically in construction and residential home maintenance, I was well-equipped to provide a range of services to clients. Then, I decided to leverage my prior experience as a handyman to establish my own business, *Peach Handyman Services*. This new venture required significant effort and dedication, but I was determined to succeed.

My Handyman Services business license.

Through resilience and hard work, I launched my business and prayed for the best. After days and nights of working diligently, my services were coming to fruition. *Peach Handyman Services* was helping me to generate sufficient income to support my family's financial, emotional, and psychological well-being.

Along with covering my wife's medical expenses, I helped with my daughter's relocation, ensuring she had a supportive environment where she could move forward and complete her dental school degree. This encouraged her to pursue her dreams and goals without feeling overburdened.

As the business grew, I could pay for my son's high school expenses, including school supplies, clothing, and other necessities. My son was able to focus on his studies and extracurricular activities without worrying about the financial implications.

Despite the challenges that I faced for days on end, the satisfaction of being able to cater to my family's needs filled me with a sense of achievement. It was a feeling of pride and fulfillment, knowing that I could provide for my loved ones despite the obstacles in our path. This sense of accomplishment gave me the strength and motivation to continue working hard. I was ready to overcome the difficulties that lay ahead.

Throughout this challenging period, I remained deeply grateful to the Almighty God for bestowing me with the strength, wisdom, intelligence, and resources necessary to overcome the adversity that threatened to engulf us. His divine guidance and grace enabled me to fulfill my responsibilities as a father and a provider of the household.

Despite the struggles, our family emerged stronger and more united than ever. Our bond was fortified by the challenges that we had overcome.

We were determined to walk through the darkness together because it meant reaching the light.

Chapter 7: My Daughter's Journey Through Dental School

"The only person you are destined to become is the person you decide to be."

-Ralph Waldo Emerson.

My beloved daughter was beginning her journey to dental school—the dream I had envisioned for myself was coming true before my eyes.

My heart swelled with love and admiration for her. It almost felt like all the hardships and struggles melted away. My daughter was about to start a new chapter that would challenge her personally and professionally. Dental College of Georgia at Augusta University wasn't for the faint-hearted, but I raised my girl with the thought process of never giving up on her dreams.

Being away from our daughter was a challenging experience for our family. The two-hour distance between our home and the Dental College meant my wife and I couldn't see her as often as we liked. We missed her presence in our daily lives, and the emptiness felt like a constant reminder of our sacrifices for her education. However, we knew this temporary separation was necessary for her growth and success. We stayed connected through regular phone calls, but nothing could replace the feeling of having her around the house.

My wife's jewelry business license after her 12 months post- surgery physical therapy.

During this time, my wife had recovered from her shoulder surgery, but the doctor had still not given her the clearance to lift heavy objects. She was asked to refrain from excessively loading her shoulder joint, as the tendons that underwent repair could re-injure her rotator cuff. However, my wife did not let her limitations stop her from starting her own business. She put her creativity to work, opened up a jewelry venture, and used her manual dexterity to craft delicate and beautiful jewelry. This entrepreneurial endeavor allowed her to visit our daughter on weekends, ensuring she felt supported despite the distance.

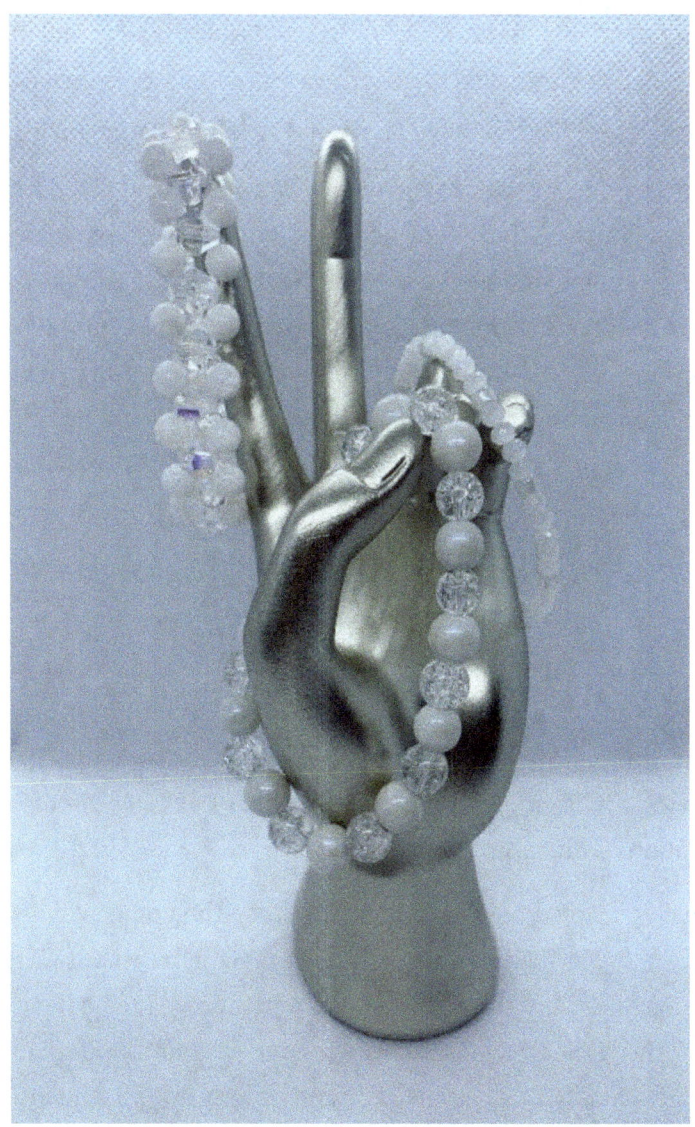

Jewelry sample made by my wife after 12 months post-surgery physical therapy.

My heart yearned to join my wife on her visits, but most of my time was spent running my business, *Handyman Services.* I worked hard to earn money for my family to provide for them and give them the support they required.

Pursuing the dental field was all my daughter wished for. Still, there were moments when the pressure to absorb vast amounts of knowledge, master intricate skills, and meet demanding deadlines felt overwhelming.

Becoming a dentist was a demanding and rigorous educational journey that required immense dedication and hard work. The four-year program was designed to equip students with the necessary knowledge, skills, and expertise to become competent and compassionate dental professionals. The curriculum included various subjects, including anatomy, biochemistry, pharmacology, and clinical dentistry. Students spend countless hours studying, attending lectures, and practicing clinical skills in simulation labs and real-world settings.

I vividly recall the day when the burden of studies overwhelmed my daughter with stress. I called her, and she poured out her heart, turning to me for advice. I encouraged and reminded her that she could achieve anything she set out to do by instilling courage, bravery, and faith in our Heavenly Father. The Holy Ghost would guide her through the arduous challenges of dental school, and soon, she would be capable of passing through the trials and tribulations with ease.

Eventually, my daughter learned to embrace the complexity of dentistry and find joy in the intricacies of the craft. The weight of responsibility, the fear of making mistakes, and the high stakes of patient care fueled her passion for excelling, driving her to push through fatigue and self-doubt. In those moments, she realized that she was exactly where she was meant to be and that her dream of becoming a dentist was within reach.

Our daughter's graduation from dental school as a General Dentist.

After a challenging four-year journey, my daughter finally graduated as a General Dentist—her graduation was the most beautiful and exciting moment in our lives.

We were immensely proud of her educational achievement, knowing how hard she had worked to pave her way to the top. Her success felt like mine, as I saw my dreams fulfilled through her accomplishments. Though I had faced many obstacles that prevented me from becoming a general dentist, my daughter had conquered the dream for both of us!

Completing my daughter's dental degree reignited my aspirations, and I saw a new path forward for our family. With my biology degree and her dental expertise, we could combine our skills to contribute to future dental practices. The passion of our shared dream of working in the dental field bloomed, and we began envisioning a future where we could work together to build a successful dental practice.

I realized that the experiences and financial resources I had accumulated as a handyman could be channeled into establishing her first dental practice. This foundation could eventually expand into a chain of dental practices, bringing our family's dream of building an economic empire in the field of dentistry to fruition.

As we looked to the future, our ambitions stretched beyond the boundaries of our home. We were determined to create a legacy to serve our community and inspire others to pursue their dreams.

Chapter 8: Reflections on Family, Education, and Life

Reflecting on my journey from Peru to the United States, the sweetest memory of my life was studying for my biology major with my daughter at Georgia State University.

From diligently spending hours to memorizing notes and graduating together, each day was filled with gratitude and adventure.

Pursuing biological sciences as a father and daughter duo was an extraordinary, unforgettable experience that deepened our bond and strengthened our family.

Each day from Monday to Friday, we would head to the university together. We took turns driving to the college, eager to chase our dreams. My daughter and I attended the same classes that the same professors instructed. We even had mutual friends!

If I had disclosed my paternal relationship with my daughter, we would become the talk of the town. I wanted my daughter to experience college like any other child instead of being subjected to undue attention. We decided not to disclose our father-daughter relationship to our classmates or teachers to avoid these potential inconveniences. It allowed us to forge our friendships and study groups while enjoying a unique, private bond only we understood.

Our days were filled with mutual support and shared learning. We studied together at the university library and at home, each teaching the other in areas where we excelled. Our dynamic as study partners was seamless, respecting the roles of father and daughter while functioning as equals in our academic pursuits. Despite maintaining our social circles at school, we always came back together as father and daughter for lunch and our drive home.

A sense of pride washed over me when we would spend hours together, cramming and studying for exams. Nothing could beat the feeling of knowing that we were high achievers and could get good grades through hard work. The shared pursuit of knowledge and growth fueled us to continue moving toward our dreams, helping us to tackle any obstacle that came our way.

After four years of hard work and dedication, our internal college faculty graduation ceremony finally arrived, and we couldn't have been more excited! Graduation day marked the culmination of our shared efforts and celebrated the unbreakable bonds we formed.

As we lined up to be recognized, my daughter approached the ceremony official, whispering that the next graduate was her father. I had no idea she had done this until my name was called.

Pride filled my heart as I watched my daughter receive her biology degree. Then, as she walked past, the official announced my name. I had graduated with honor distinction, Magna Cum Laude—I couldn't believe it!

Before I could fully process this prestigious moment, the announcer shared that I was the father of the previous graduate. The realization of our unique "father-daughter bond" dawned on everyone present, and the audience erupted in applause.

The outpouring of congratulations and admiration from fellow graduates, my family, and friends was overwhelming, marking one of the most exhilarating moments of our lives. Everyone we knew was left speechless; they couldn't believe that my daughter and I had graduated together with immense grace!

My dedication to education and hard work was deeply rooted in the example set by my parents. Growing up in Peru, my father worked tirelessly and pursued higher education, graduating as a philosophy and social sciences professor. My mother took care of us when we were young and continued to pursue her studies, eventually becoming a skilled dressmaker. My parent's sacrifices and commitment instilled in me the value of devoting oneself to studying and diligently working to provide for the family's economic needs. For this reason, I have always believed in the importance of education in overcoming challenges, gaining security, and earning respect.

Throughout my life, I juggled studying, managing financial responsibilities, working as a handyman, and spending quality time with my family. I realized that achieving one's goals required adapting to a balanced lifestyle, so I consciously prioritized my time, allocating it wisely between academics, work, family, and personal enjoyment. This balanced approach taught me that a healthy lifestyle was not only about achieving success but also nurturing relationships, fostering personal growth, and finding joy in the little moments.

None of my dreams would have been possible without the unwavering support of my wife. She shared the responsibilities that came our way and encouraged me to follow the ideas that I had envisioned. Throughout our lives, we made time for travel, explored Peru and various parts of the United

States, and created memories that strengthened our bond and broadened our perspectives.

Despite the occasional economic difficulties, our resilience in trying times and careful saving habits ensured that we were prepared for life's challenges. This stability allowed us to support our children's educational aspirations and witness their remarkable achievements. Our shared efforts have left a lasting impact on their personal and professional lives.

My son is currently working as a biomedical scientist and pursuing a master's degree. He aspires to continue his doctorate in scientific data analysis once his master's is complete. As for his personal life, he tied the knot in 2020 and has purchased a three-floor house with his wife. She is a food scientist by profession and is enthusiastic about working in the field. My daughter-in-law is expecting their first child, a baby girl, and we cannot wait to welcome our grandchild in 2024!

Meanwhile, my daughter is a successful general dentist and married a computer engineer in 2023. She will also welcome her first child, a baby girl, and we are excited to welcome another grandchild in 2024! She plans to open her dental practice relatively soon, in 2025.

My children's successes reflect the educational legacy that my parents imparted to me, which I passed on to them.

Our journey has inspired our extended family and relatives to pursue nursing and other professional careers.

By the grace of God, the ripple effect of our commitment to education and hard work will continue to influence the generations that are to come.

I am profoundly grateful to my Heavenly Father for guiding me to the United States, for the opportunity to learn English, for my professional accomplishments in biology, and for the respect I have earned in this blessed country.

I am thankful for every blessing that has made me and my family into who we are today.

Conclusion: From Personal to Public

Several factors compelled me to share my personal life or an inspirational story with the public, even though it contains happiness and sadness, accomplishments and setbacks, laughter and tears, and errors and lessons learned.

Throughout my life, I discovered how to confront life's obstacles with bravery, sagacity, modesty, and affection.

A personal endeavor that I undertook was to diligently develop into the following roles: a devoted father to my children, an exemplary spouse who cherishes and honors his spouse, a reliable son who attends to the needs of his parents, a thoughtful grandfather to my prospective grandchildren, and a model for my generation as a whole.

Although I acknowledge that I have not achieved perfection, I derive satisfaction from my positive contributions to my family. Leaving an educational legacy for my entire generation fills me with the utmost satisfaction.

I possess an intense aspiration to motivate individuals to engage in constructive endeavors that have the potential to revolutionize both our localities and the global community.

To those reading this, I want to extend a heartfelt message of encouragement—pursue higher education, face life's challenges head-on, and never give up on your dreams.

I have shared my personal experiences not just to tell *my* story but to inspire others to open up about *their* own hardships.

If I can overcome adversity and achieve my dreams, so can you.

Although my initial objective was to earn a dental degree alongside my daughter, life's challenges compelled me to prioritize my children's and my spouse's well-being over my interests. Nevertheless, I completed my post-secondary education.

As a biologist, I am content with my profession because it provides me with stability and prospects for employment in any location; in fact, there is a perpetual demand for individuals with an academic background.

In addition, possessing a university degree as a professional brings credibility and societal respect. It allows the competent authorities to treat us with dignity and diligently attend to our needs. Education instills a sense of belonging and highlights our significance in society.

This recognition and support have motivated me to continue pushing boundaries and striving for excellence in my work. I am proud to be part of a community that values and respects the contributions of its members.

Prestige enables us to confront every challenge in life with assurance, skill, wisdom, and caution. It fosters feelings of security and high regard.

For this reason, I wish to inspire young adults, middle-aged adults, and late adults who could not attend university to pursue an academic career that will boost their confidence and increase their financial prospects. **There is no limit to your dreams, and age is not a barrier.**

The benefits of higher education are endless, but most importantly, academic excellence will help you influence your children and your family to make decisions that serve them well in the future, ensuring their economic safety and prosperity.

By setting an example and demonstrating the benefits of academic achievement, you can positively influence future generations in your family. Your decision to pursue higher education can pave the way for a more secure and prosperous future for yourself and your loved ones.

When I revealed my academic achievements and stories filled with positivity to my friends and neighbors, I received compliments describing my inspirational moments in life as remarkable, exemplary, and truly unique.

Remarkably, my acquaintances and neighbors recommended that I circulate my narrative to the general public to inspire and motivate people worldwide to pursue higher education and strengthen familial bonds.

I contemplated sharing my personal experiences with the world, and one day, while returning home from college via the freeway, I encountered a police car that pursued me. The officer's lights eventually came on, forcing me to stop and pull over.

The officer inquired where I was coming from, stating that I exceeded the speed limit by fifteen miles. I told him I was returning home from Georgia State University, where I was a student.

He subsequently questioned what I was studying, and after a ten-minute conversation about my collegiate pursuits, including my role as a study partner for my daughter, he was shocked!

The officer suggested I share my educational story with the world. In the end, he issued a warning rather than a speeding ticket! I couldn't believe my eyes.

As a result, the overwhelmingly positive feedback I received after sharing my motivational story with others prompted me to consider the possibility of penning a book detailing my life. I ultimately chose to expand upon my book to increase its exposure to a national and international audience.

Since my daughter was born, my duty was to ensure her safety and well-being, instilling a sense of assurance that encouraged her toward self-development. I have strived to teach my daughter resilience and perseverance in the face of challenges. These qualities have helped her navigate life's obstacles with confidence and grace.

Our shared academic experience is my way of showing my unconditional love for her. It demonstrates that my unwavering emotional support strengthens my daughter's life.

I believe that as a father, it is incumbent upon me to act as an exemplar, imparting profound life lessons, establishing fundamental values, and empowering my children to confront the trials and tribulations that arise.

When my children were in their last year of high school, I supported them and advised them to make their own decisions to determine their aspirations.

I served as a role model by actively participating in my children's growth and development, helping to establish a strong foundation for their interpersonal connections, and contributing to the cultivation of positive emotional intelligence in them.

My daughter's accomplishments are proof of my positive influence on her personal development and academic success. She graduated from Georgia State University with me and had complete faith in her ability to succeed in college. Later, in May 2021, she received her general dentistry degree from the Dental College of Georgia. I am proud to have shaped her into the confident and capable woman she is today.

Furthermore, my supporting role as a father benefited my son's self-sufficiency and personal confidence. I am proud to have shaped him into the self-reliant and confident individual he is today.

Reflecting on the journey that has led me to this point, I am filled with gratitude and accomplishment.

The path has not been without its challenges. Still, through perseverance, faith, and my family's unwavering love and support, I have overcome adversity and achieved remarkable success.

My story is about the incredible power of education, the strength we draw from our families, and how life can change for the better when we diligently follow our dreams. I want to share my journey to inspire others, especially young people, to pursue higher education and treasure the precious bonds within their families.

I hope my experiences can light the way for others, showing that the future holds endless possibilities and the chance to reach one's full potential. Even with my flaws, I'm humbled by the positive impact I've had on my loved ones, and this motivates me to keep making a meaningful difference in their lives.

This is my legacy—*one that I hope will echo through the generations, transcend over time, and inspire others to achieve greatness.*

My son working as a biomedical scientist in the field of Biomedical Science.

Spending a good time at Disney World in Orlando, Florida, with my family. I ensured that we focused on education and providing our children with the best childhood.

Lima, Peru.

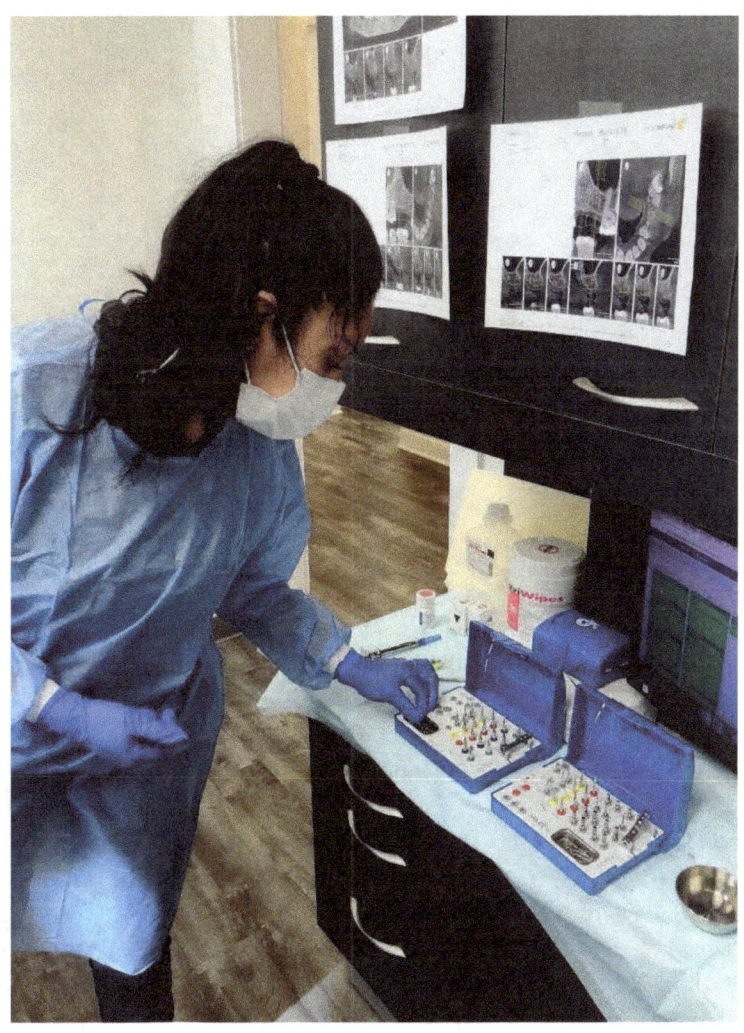

My daughter, working as a general dentist. This is an example of the lasting impact of my dedication on the family's educational aspirations (enduring legacy).

Disney World in Orlando, Florida.

www.ingramcontent.com/pod-product-compliance
Lightning Source LLC
Chambersburg PA
CBHW070643130626
46555CB00006B/2684